ARTHRITIS AND ME

An Inspirational Story

MONIQUE MCKENZIE

authorHOUSE

AuthorHouse™
1663 Liberty Drive
Bloomington, IN 47403
www.authorhouse.com
Phone: 1 (800) 839-8640

© 2016 Monique McKenzie. All rights reserved.

Proofread by: Deborah Hardwick

No part of this book may be reproduced, stored in a retrieval system, or transmitted by any means without the written permission of the author.

Published by AuthorHouse 06/30/2016

ISBN: 978-1-5049-8633-5 (sc)
ISBN: 978-1-5049-8631-1 (hc)
ISBN: 978-1-5049-8632-8 (e)

Library of Congress Control Number: 2016904745

Print information available on the last page.

Any people depicted in stock imagery provided by Thinkstock are models, and such images are being used for illustrative purposes only. Certain stock imagery © Thinkstock.

This book is printed on acid-free paper.

Because of the dynamic nature of the Internet, any web addresses or links contained in this book may have changed since publication and may no longer be valid. The views expressed in this work are solely those of the author and do not necessarily reflect the views of the publisher, and the publisher hereby disclaims any responsibility for them.

My Precious Readers

This book was written to inspire the sick, the healthy,
    And so we can learn to live each day to its maximum potential;
        To inflate your heart and mind to the extreme
            And to love one another, as if it is your last day on this
                Beautiful earth.

For the loving memory of my Grandfather a.k.a "Big Daddy:"

Alvin McKenzie

Who have always instilled the *importance of education* to your
Children, Grand-Children, and Great Grand-Children.
Our family will continue to plant the seed that you've given us,
by allowing that seed to grow inside of every child and young adult.
Continually, we will strive in making a
difference in this world we live in,
because of the lessons that you have taught us.

To my brother:

Shaunn ParKinson

Who has suffered through life with an illness, since adolescents
and continues to always remain strong.
You are the true meaning of *ABLE* and I love you with all my heart.
Continue to strive for success
and don't let anyone tell you different.

To My Strong and Successful Readers:

The past teaches
The Future is your destiny for which only you can create
I walk to see people struggling for a dollar, but are comfortable
who am I to judge
I have plans and so do you
Don't give up on your dreams
Write them down, Stop procrastinating
and continue living to turn those dreams into a reality
"Think.Dream.Reality."
Be who you were meant to be
Who are you?
A Successful Goal Driven Individual, No Matter the Cause!

-Monique McKenzie-

Contents

Preface xv
Introduction xvii

Chapter 1   How This Diagnosis Changed My Life 1
Chapter 2   Coping with Arthritis 7
Chapter 3   This is Me 21
Chapter 4   College Life 27
Chapter 5   Life's Existence 33
Chapter 6   My Hardships 41
Chapter 7   Good Relationship or NOT! 47
Chapter 8   Turning Point (Reunited In Peace)
            As Brooklyn remain in Heaven 51
Chapter 9   Becoming an Aspiration to Be an Inspiration 59
Chapter 10 What I Have Learned 65
Chapter 11 (The Final Destination) My Career 69

Acknowledgements 77

To the Arthritis Foundation

For fighting for the arthritis community and providing information and resources to individuals so we may live a fulfilling life.

www.arthritis.org

Preface

Arthritis and Me came about to inspire young adults to never give up on their dreams and goals, or who has struggled with an illness and are looking for answers on dealing with life changes. I have been through many ups and downs throughout the years, but at the end of the day, this was just lessons learned, the knowledge that needed to be kept, and dreams that needed to be fulfilled. I have struggled with being a single parent at age 20 and continuously helping and motivating others when I could barely help myself. I suffered through bad relationships and hanging out with the wrong crowd, which resulted in me losing my way. It was clear to me, and very much understood where I wanted to go in life, but I wasn't certain on how to access that motive to further better myself. I gained experiences along the way with certain jobs with the opportunity of becoming promoted to higher positions. My setback was always listening to others tell me how to live my life, instead of figuring out what worked best for my child and I.

My dreams always been to become a part of the entertainment industry since I was a little girl. A couple of years ago, I went through a tragic experience, which caused me to becoming depressed, gain an accessible amount of weight, and not to mention stress. This led me to want to work hard and set goals for myself.

Now I have started my own business as well as finishing my degree in college. It took me awhile, but I finally woke up to know what life truly had to offer, besides lying around in self-pity. My story is to allow readers to understand the importance of following your dreams and goals and sticking to them, no matter the cause. Don't let anything, such as an illness, stop you from achieving; Do not allow yourself to waste precious time with people who are holding you back, whether it is friends or family; although, moral support can be a huge help when needed. Focus on yourself and what is best for you. THINK ABOUT IT!!! Do not allow anyone to tell you different and just listen to your inner voice. Trust me when I say, anything that can disrupt your future goals will always be there. I waited quite awhile to make something happen. At one point, I did not think I could do it, only because of an illness; I am just stopping you from doing the same. We all know the difference between thinking of doing it and doing the actual. Let us all become an inspiration and a guide for other individuals to do the same.

Monique Mckenzie
Houston, TX
July 2015

Introduction

Are you where you want to be in life, currently? Are certain obstacles in your life getting in your way of accomplishing your future goals? Think back real hard and ask yourself these questions. Well, what are you going to do about it? Everyone goes through their own difficulties in life and it is up to you to fix the situation in order to succeed. Education is a start and very important to have; especially in this day and time.

We all want to have fun and experience the adventures of going to parties and engaging ourselves around the wrong people, all because of the pleasurable circumstances. Stop and think! Are the group of people you surround yourself around really your friends? It is very important to look out for your best interest. All friends are not good friends. Follow what your future dreams and goals are and you will encompass yourself with other driven individuals. Do not allow your friends to pressure you into something you have no business pursuing. Hint: I'm talking about your so-called buddies or partners in crime, literally! Before you know it: 5, 10, and 15 years would have passed and you are just sitting there like a *duck* with the same group of ducklings who are no longer going anywhere with their lives as well. This kind of behavior will continue to hold you back from achieving your own aspirations. Do not allow time to pass you by. Believe me, these years are going and are not stopping or slowing down for anyone. Friends come and go, but your education will be there to provide you a better future. Which one would you choose? I hope *education and most importantly, it starts with You!* There is nothing wrong with having a break and wanting to just get out, only to continue on with what you are destined to do right after. Don't allow yourself to ever give up or even say that you can't do it or don't know where to start. Think! If you have an important meeting to attend that will benefit you in the long run, are you going to chill with your homies or take care of business? *Stop Procrastinating! Procrastinating* is the worst thing you could do. All of these are just excuses and there are people who are willing to help, such as counselors, your family, church, members, teachers, or even friends who are on that same path. Lead by example and I promise you that others that want the same for themselves will follow. Inspire other young adults and even children to do the same so that they may also have a promising future and will look to you as their mentor. Our world is changing and it is our job as individuals to make our communities a better and fearless place for us to live in. You cannot help others who do not want to be helped; as long as you tried, that's all that matters. *"Become an aspiration to be an inspiration!"* Continue to the chapters of this book and become inspired by a true story of my life and how I managed an illness along with struggles which lead me to wake up and smell the coffee, for a better and promising future for myself, my health, and my child.

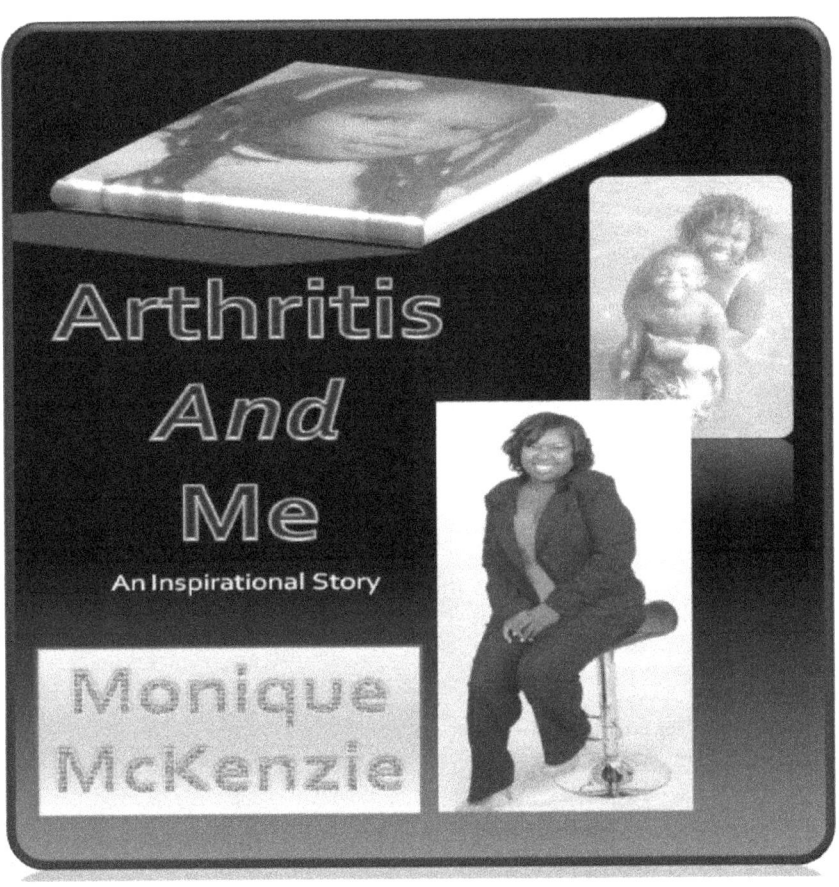

CHAPTER 1

How This Diagnosis Changed My Life

I was only six years old; February 1992. I remember; it was my childhood best friend, Sammie and I. Sammie would always come over to my house so we could play outside. We always enjoyed the entertainment of jumping, climbing, and my favorite thing to do was the old-fashioned cartwheels, where you flew your hands in the air, flipped on over, and landed on your feet without falling or stumbling over and maintaining our balance.

My name is Monica Mckinley and I was raised with my mother Elizabeth Mckinley, my older sister Rebecca, and my aunt Stephany, which is my mother's youngest sister. We stayed in Ft. Lauderdale, FL with our darling grandmother. In the meantime, my mother stayed in New York so that she was able to complete her bachelor's degree in nursing. Once finished, my mother came back for us for the move to Houston, TX, where other members of our family lived. We lived in a 2 bedroom townhome and at that time I was in 1st grade where I had met Sammie; we both went to the same elementary school and stayed only a block away from each other. I had a wonderful babysitter, named Joy who was such a sweetheart and allowed me to play outside most of the time, instead of staying indoors with nothing to do, as long as my homework and chores were completed. One day while playing outside with bestie Sammie; we were once again entertaining each other as always. We had noticed a carpenter table that was surrounded by two big trees across the street from the townhome where we once lived. Sammie and I ran over towards the table to get a good glimpse and were determined to jump on and off numerous times.

While playing continuously around the table, I went ahead and made a last attempt to jump one more time and fell straight down on my right ankle, and landed right on the gray concrete sidewalk. All my weight from my body immediately fell upon this one ankle. I received a sudden rush of pain and could not move at all; it was almost like a brick had slammed down with extreme pressure pulling further and further on my foot. In this case, my body along with my foot actually hit to the floor of the concrete. I could hardly breathe while crying profusely. My first panic attack. I was the type that was really sensitive to pain, so sensitive that I would sob even if the pain was minor. I would get embarrassed so easily even if I had the tiniest booboo, especially when others were around that witnessed the situation that had occurred. As my ankle continued hurting and becoming overwhelmed with pain, you could imagine what was going on in my head. I just wanted my "mommy."

While lying there in distraught, Sammie was so worried and confused at the same time and ran to get help from my babysitter, Joy. I had watched Joy and Sammie running towards me anxious and trying to figure out what was wrong. I made an attempt to try and explain, while crying out loudly, with tears running down my face, and Joy attempting to slowly pick me up and take me to the house. I just watched Sammie look at me from behind us with the hope of being okay while we carefully walked away. Joy immediately contacted my mother when we made it to the house to inform her of what had just happened. My mother did not think too much of it and went ahead and advised Joy to give me some Motrin, which should take care of the pain. As I waited patiently for the pain to subside; one hour, two hours, three hours, nothing, not even a flicker. I was still in excruciating pain and not to mention my right ankle that I sprung became warm as if it had a 102.5 temperature living inside of it, and not to mention it was extremely swollen and throbbing like a soft kiddie football; Yes! Just like that.

When my mother came home, she would continue to give me Motrin every four to six hours as stated on the bottle, well in her case every four hours, not to exceed five pills within a 24 hour period. When it became night time, I started sweating horrifically. I would be so drenched in sweat to the point where I began having sleepless nights and tossing, turning all night while my ankle was still in pain and full of watery fluid. I started becoming dehydrated, so it was important for my mother to ensure that I drink a lot of water and Gatorade to replace all the electrolytes and gain the energy that I had lost from sweating too much. I had to sleep with my mother so that she was able to keep an eye on me and make certain that I was alright, and if the symptoms would progress accordingly. As for me, I was only six, my mother and I was not sure of the nature of my condition, only that my foot hurt so badly, and made it impossible for me to walk on, let alone find my way to the bathroom. My mother tried everything down to ice packs, cold baths, Bengay, and Pain Killers, nothing appeared to work. The pain would surpass for a short period of time but return within a matter of minutes, still swelling, and continuously throbbing if I made any attempts to push or glide against a solid surface with this painful ankle. After about three days, my mother called the ambulance to come pick me up and I was transported to Plantation Hospital shortly after, where

I was stuck in the emergency room for 24 hours or more; while the on-call physician and nurses tried coming to a conclusion as to why my ankle was in such bad shape. I was given I.V.'s in my arm and had to be given a dose of strong pain shots to get the pain and swelling to go down, which only helped temporarily.

While at the hospital, the doctors and nurses could not really figure out what the issue was regarding this pain and swelling in my joints and because I was a child I required special attention with the right equipment and the right physicians. I was again transported to a Children's Hospital so that I was able to receive the care that I needed. At that time, I am looking so confused asking the Why's and How's on so many occasions is this happening to me. I did not understand, I was only six turning seven in a few months. Like the other hospital I had to receive another stick in the arm for IV access. Since the physicians could not figure out the "Why" in what was going on with me and the How. Child Protective Services (CPS) had got involved asking my mother various questions regarding my condition and how it occurred, just to make sure there was no act of domestic violence inside our home. I guess they were just doing their job, especially when it came to the children in need of serious medical attention. There were nurses coming in and out of the room to perform various blood work and conduct x-rays on my ankle, to figure what the cause of these symptoms were.

The medical professionals checked for all different types of diseases such as Cancer, Bone Marrow, and of course, Arthritis was the last testing that was done. Until the verdict was made, the physicians had injected me with a penicillin shot in my hip to bring the swelling and pain down while figuring out what became the basis of this issue. When I saw the needle, I almost passed out; it was long and thick filled with fluid. I screamed in fear and pain so loudly that all the patients, nurses, and doctors outside and down the hall could hear me. I had to have four nurses hold me down while they stuck me in my hips in multiple places. I cried and I bawled, I wanted out! I just wanted to revolve back to playing with my friends, so that everything could be back to normal like it was before. Although this was going on, it also was a detrimental experience that caused my mother to miss out on several days of work and for me to miss out on several days of school; which forced me to become held back from school for one year. After several days of being in the hospital; I was referred to a Rheumatologist who was affiliated with the Children's Hospital. The doctor I had to immediately start seeing was a physician who treated and managed patients with arthritis and other *rheumatic diseases*. It was indeed a known fact that I had what is called Juvenile Rheumatoid Arthritis (JRA).

Of course, I had no perceptive of what Arthritis was, which induced me to go along with my everyday life with the thought of acting as though there was no illness infused inside of me and that I was still as normal as other children. My Rheumatologist prescribed me with prednisone, which was a steroidal drug used to treat inflammation, such as swelling and prevent pain in joints due to the *Arthritis*. The only major fact when taking steroids, is that it causes you to have excessive weight gain, which was not healthy for my joints at all. The more weight I gain the more immobile I had become which was never an option for me. I was given Methotrexate to control the inflammation, which had extreme side effects that could caused liver damage; because of that I had to get my blood checked every month to make sure there were no changes to my liver. Furthermore, I had what is called Thalassemia Anemia which is a lower than normal red blood cells or the cause of not having enough protein inside them to fulfill suitable energy to get through the day. With having Thalassemia I have to take Folic Acid which is an iron vitamin that allows your body to produce and make new cells that prevent me from having cancer or producing cancerous-like cells. If you ever heard of anyone that has any type of anemia, you should also know that it can allow you to become tired and restless. Sometimes I would even become cold one minute and then hot the next. With everything that I had going on, my Rheumatologist did not make it much easier when he informed my mother that I would not be able to walk at the age of 15 and that I would have to be in a wheelchair for the rest of my entity. At this moment, I was only able to try and live my life as normal as possible or at least what was left of it.

CHAPTER 2

Coping with Arthritis

August of 1992, I had to repeat the first-grade because I was kept in the hospital for weeks due to the JRA and all the medications that I was given I was not able to catch up on all my school work in time. I still did not know or understand what JRA was and how it even occurred. All I remember was jumping on and off that table with my friend and "BOOM" there it was "ARTHRITIS," "What? How is this even possible?" I thought. My mother believed this could even possibly come from being in daycare with other kids spreading nasty germs around. The truth is there has not yet been a solution to how children are being diagnosed with JRA and has not been a reasonable cure settled for it either. In spite of everything, the anticipation in my head was believed to be that I was indeed still normal as they come, excluding all the medications that I was given. This did not mean much to me at the time. I was even told by my mother and doctor to take it easy and make sure to have plenty of rest. "Yea, sure!" I was seven, so what did that mean to me? But be a kid and have fun, fun, and more fun. I still performed in activities in P.E. with *no problem*; I could run with my friends with *no problem*, and even ride my bike with *no problem*.

I was unstoppable, could no one tell me to take it easy! Please! Arthritis meant nothing to me.

While acting like a normal seven-year-old child, one day while in P.E. we had several stations that each child had to engage in. We had to do rock climbing, rope climbing, back flips, kicking balls through cones, and so forth. I never mastered rope climbing, but everything else was a piece of cake!

Since my diagnosis with JRA, this became a challenge for the first time to test my inner strengths. My P.E. teacher was well aware of my illness and wanted to make sure it was okay to participate in such activities. I responded by saying, "yes, there is nothing wrong with me, that's easy." If you haven't noticed, I was a very determined child, who thought she was invincible. As I approached the back flipping station and begun kneeling carefully, trying not to lose balance on the long, blue, firm mat, and suddenly looking downward in reassurance as if something was not right. At this moment, right away, Immediately, I started feeling fear with an ounce of uncertainty. I could not put a finger on it, but all of a sudden my emotions had arisen and I started to second guess this back-flipping situation; as I am now feeling a little shaky and in almost, but the not quite deep desperation of maybe this idea was not such a good idea after all. At this time, I felt that I could not just turn back and tell my P.E. teacher that I have a change of heart and I just can't do this after I had already told her I could. It was this little thing in me called, "pride." This was the first time since I was diagnosed with JRA that I did a flip. It was now all up to me to see what will happen next.

My mother and doctor expressed to me how serious my condition was and that there was going to be limitations to my joints over time. It's not that I didn't believe them. I just still wasn't sure of what they meant by that, since I was too young to comprehend what or how arthritis will affect me from this day forward. Let me clarify some things: Who goes from being able to do almost anything as a kid to doing basically nothing while you just sit there and watch everyone else having a good time being as mobile as they can possibly be with no worries or concerns about their limitations; this wasn't me. Anyways, while kneeling down into a turtle shell position to do this so-called flip, I firmly pushed my legs up to start my turnover. As my legs and knees left the ground and all my body weight started to apply pressure to my head with the feeling of the blood flow rushing down towards my skull; the thought in my mind as if "I got this!" Making this attempt to hold my weight as I was slowly and steadily coming on to the other side with my legs in the air and my foot steadily losing balance hitting the mat that didn't seem so firm after all; it was hard and fast…"BOOM! POP!" my eyes automatically started to bulge out in alarm and distress mode. The pain, the pain, "OUCH!" Tears immediately fell down my face; everything went silent and my only focus and concern were the pain in my lower back, "POP!" The other kids looked as if they were moving in slow motion and all eyes were on me filled with so many worries and the atmosphere in the room seemed gloomy. Talk about an embarrassment; this has never happened to me before. The pain was so excruciating. It took me back to the first time when I jumped off the table before my diagnosis of JRA and again that same feeling occurred with the continuance of hyperventilation as if my lungs were closing in on me; it was a form of a panic attack. My P.E. teacher looked at me in fear like my friend Sammie did as she tried to help me. I yelled out to her with filling tears of destitution, "NOOO!" I never meant to scream at her, I was just so perpetually ashamed of the fact that I got hurt in front of my classmates, and could not point out what the kids were thinking of me right now or how they were feeling watching me lying here in pain. Yes! This absolutely became the start of an ultimate problem for me. The P.E. teacher had given one of the students permission to hurry and run over and get the school nurse while I stayed in her care. My vision became blurry and it looked as if I was in a dreamy state of mind, as my head was tilted back to look and see the nurse coming towards me with a wheelchair. At that moment, I started to realize how serious the JRA was and had finally came to begin to have a slight understanding of what my mother and doctor meant when they said, "take it easy." It was time to slow my role.

As the nurse came to get me from P.E. and took me back to the nurse's office, she provided me with some pain medicine while allowing me to lay down on the bed for about 45 minutes to an hour until I was okay to go back to class. I stood there while laying down looking at the walls in the dark room where I was laying, thinking to myself how something was not right and I cried and I cried while laying in the bed in total distress. I was finally able to fall asleep and wake up as if it was all one big messed up nightmare. I started feeling different than the other kids and would sit or stand to watch them perform cartwheels, backflips, jumping, skipping, climbing trees with a sickening smile on their face, just happy and filled with glee! You could always tell when a person is having a good day. Me, I just felt alone and in total destruction!

Later as time went on and I went into 2nd grade, my mother, sister, aunt, and I moved away from the area where we lived and moved into a three-bedroom house. I was transferred to another elementary school and we moved into a three bedroom house. I received physical and speech therapy, not to mention riding the yellow short bus to school. I mean where they pick you up in front of the house and drop you off in front of the school, and vice-versa. Transferring to a different school where I did not know anybody was a big challenge for me; I had already gained so much weight due to the steroids that I was currently taking, which shown on my face; this was everyone's playground; those chubby cheeks of mine, I hated them! Yeah, that "moon face" is what they call it. This all came from taking steroid medications; which really sucked.

Through my years of going to elementary and middle school, I was continuously made fun of by this kid named Jeremy, who was not America's Superstar himself. He was tall, dark skinned, and had peacock legs that looked as if they never seen lotion or knew what lotion was. Although that was the case, his words still cut deep. I was called "fatty," "chipmunk," "ugly," "crippled," and other names he felt like calling me, depending on what day it was or the kind of day he was having. I never allowed Jeremy's hurtful words overpower me because I would just either make fun back or not pay him any attention and just say, "whatever" while moving on to something that was more constructive than dealing with a loser like him or any other tribes that wanted to join in on his foolish ways just to be cool. I was not the only person that was included in his stupid tactics. My friend Sasha who was the only one I hung with also would get trapped into Jeremy's horrible defense. However, one day Jeremy was having a ball, I mean just cracking jokes on Sasha and me and we plotted and chose to go outside with a pair of scissors and flatten his tires on his bicycle right after the last bell rang. This was our motive; we had to get back at him for his cruelty towards us. After awhile, I did indeed become very vengeful, due to all the teasing and disrespectful comments from Jeremy; since this was the only way of defending myself and people I cared about. I believed what you do to me, be sure to expect the same, or maybe even worse in return. Sasha and I could not wait until the school bell rang for us to go to the bus so we could watch Jeremy squirm seeing his bike on flat. While watching Jeremy walk to his bike and Sasha and I peeking around the corner, the look on his face was hilarious. We were thinking to ourselves, "that'll show him to mess with anyone again." Little did we know, he came back the next day with a new tire on his bike or maybe he had got the hole plugged; I don't know. I mean he could not possibly just have a spare bicycle tire hanging around in his garage. Uuuugh! I began to become frustrated and plot against other ways I could get back at him. I even thought to punch a hole in his bicycle tire again; only because I was curious about what will happen the next day just to see if Jeremy would come with another tire once again.

Meanwhile, as time went by in middle school, things got a little better besides dealing with the idiot, Jeremy. Unlike other young girls, I started my menstrual cycle in my 8th grade school year. I thought that was kind of late from what I hear girls can start their cycle anywhere from nine to 13 years old. After a few months of seeing my period, I started having major flare-ups with my arthritis. My joints could barely move and were once again warm and swollen. The flare-up started again at my ankles and worked its way up towards the rest of my joints throughout my body; such as my arms, wrists and so forth. This is what my mother and doctor tried to explain to me about my condition progressing and limiting my mobility. I would take hot baths and pain medicine to ease the pain but for some reason, this did not work. With having these so-called flare-ups, I was hoping this was not the end of somewhat a normal life since my doctor seemed so certain that I will be in a wheelchair at the age of 15.

My mother and I went to the Medical Center that was not too far from our house and told them to go ahead and admit me in the hospital and give me plenty of fluids to increase my immune system and minimize the dehydration. Since my mother was a nurse professional, she always ensures that I was able to receive the right kind of care I needed and nine out of 10 times she will just tell them what I need. Got to love her! Because most of the times when you go into an emergency room and if you are not physically looking like you need intensive medical attention, they will usually diagnose you with anything and prescribe you some pain meds, and tell you to follow up with a doctor in a few days and send you on your way; my mother wasn't going for that and needed to make sure I was able to get back in my usual condition. Anyways, once again back to the hospital, I go. There is an IV in my arm and again with the steroid medication that had to be given so I could get better. I thought I was perfectly okay and healthy since my diagnosis, now nine years later this "flare-up" decided to come along, "uuuuugh!" I guess it had to do more with the hormones in my body changing, because of the fact I started my cycle, I assume! My period even stopped the month of me having the flare-up and my mother thought I had been having sex and got pregnant. Little did she know, I was still a virgin and anyone who knew me also knew that I was too shy to even get close to a guy, better yet talk to one unless it was on a friendly connection to where that was nowhere close to my mind. It was brought to my attention that if I got sick, stressed, or had any types of infection or hormonal changes; these are only some of the few things that can cause a flare-up to happen and possibly allow my period cycle to stop or become late. The trigger was the flu that occurred around the winter season; this was somewhere around New Years. I ended up staying in the hospital for a couple of days and even got to sit in one of their relaxing hot bubbly bathtubs that the hospital provided to their patients. This was very relaxing and I got to work out my joints while in there.

After being discharged from the hospital, I felt a lot better and I was still walking and moving around as normal. I was going to be perfectly fine, in which I believed it to be. I really started accepting my diagnosis around my high school years, well maybe just a little acceptance. In middle school, I started making more friends and just a few enemies along the way even if I did not know they were my enemies because of my sweet and genuine personality. I loved everyone and was always happy. What could little old me do to anyone? When I did finally reached middle school, I had to beg and plead to my mother to stop me from riding the short yellow school bus. Growing up, I have always been convinced that there was nothing wrong with me. Although as time went on, I started noticing my joints becoming more and more inflamed and stiff, especially during the cold weather throughout my whole body. I was not able to straighten my arms and bend my knees all the way or even turn my neck all the way to a 90 degree angle. I could go upstairs, downstairs, run, and sometimes climb depending on what it was I had to climb. Yes! I do have certain limitations, but I was a strong-willed kid and would try anything just to prove to everyone how normal I was. I was not stupid. I was an A and B student and I could perform in certain extracurricular activities, but not all, and that was "okay." I was so normal that I even tried out for the new dance team in 7th grade. Again, I did have certain limitations and was hoping the dance teachers did not notice, but at least I tried is what I would always say. I would warm-up and do the dance moves the same, because I have always loved to dance; this was my passion growing up as a kid. I enjoyed singing and dancing to R&B and old school jams since the age of zero; I just knew this would be my career when I got older, because I could never stop breaking out a dance move; especially if it came from a song I really knew or loved. When it came to the final decision on who got accepted on the dance team; a lot of names were being called. As I was patiently waiting on mines and watching others with their sleeves on their shoulders and a "congratulations" for making the team. Others who didn't make the team received, *"Thank you to everyone who tried out. Those who didn't make it, you are more than welcome to try again next year."* They announced. Again my heart was filled with disappointment.

I went home crying to my mother and so torn. My eyes were red, my vision became blurry, and I could barely breathe. When you are used to being flexible and have been so active for seven years and then all of a sudden it all gets taken away from you; it is a very devastating and a tragic feeling, to watch everyone do all the things I used to once do.

Meanwhile, things started looking up for me when I got to high school. I had to transfer from the high school that I started to attend from middle school to a whole new district in another part of town where I did not know anyone. I met a few students once I became registered and who were nice enough to show me around the school and were extra friendly. You could tell by the looks of the surrounding who was part of the popular crowd. The students who assisted me to get settled in my classes and show me where my locker was located, was there to do just that. If I sat with one of the students who helped me in finding my classes during lunch break, I would be under the impression that we were off to a great start and I possibly had a friend. Sometimes they would feel a certain way of new students, especially Freshman's who joined the school and call them "FISH" or "Fresh Meat" which is a term for new students who were just starting out or who was enrolled as a new student.

Later on, I started becoming a little more comfortable with having Rheumatoid Arthritis and I started to share that information with others who were curious on why I had special accommodations such as: why my test answers were only A, B, C and not A, B, C, D, or why I was either limping or why everyone would sit on the floor and I had to sit on a chair, and I also had to take speech therapy to improve on my talking skills as well. There were other students who would sometimes stare at the way I walk and would notice me limping and would make fun of it, but I would just look, laugh, and think they were stupid; it never seemed to bother me, only just a little bit, but it didn't really matter;

what could me or anyone else do to stop them? They were stupid, naïve, and probably failing *Physical Education*. Sometimes instead of telling the other students that I had arthritis, I would just say that my legs hurt or I twisted it or some type of lame excuse to get them off my back. Questions, regarding my diagnosis, was no one's business and didn't deserve any kind of explanation. "Be glad it is not you that have it." Is what I would always say. As I did get older, in the back of my head was the question, why me? What did I do to deserve this? And, the people that don't have it and have this inconspicuous evil mentality to make fun of others, I would feel as if they should have this and not me. This is just how I began to feel, during the high school years. My mother has three kids and I would wonder why I became the chosen to one to be diagnosed with arthritis. Nothing ever seemed fair to me at all, but it was LIFE and I had no choice but to deal with it and *just deal with it!*

I had my first boyfriend in high school or shall I say a friendly crush. If you ever lived in my household with my mother; a boyfriend was not possible to have, they couldn't even call my house or I would need to have some type of explanation, and if they did call, it better be about school. This so-called relationship did not last too long anyways because he was more interested in what was in his pants than getting to know me as a person. He asked me one day if I could go to the movies with him at 9:00pm on a school night. I told him that was not possible and he broke up with me the next day. Oh, the "irony." I knew from that little tiny incident that relationships were nothing but a "no go." This was the start of me knowing what boys were all about.

During high school I was not able to join in any sports because of my condition, but I did join in organizations to keep myself involved and active, such as: The Minority Heritage Club (MHC), Future Business Leaders of America (FBLA), Health Occupation Students of America (HOSA), Culinary Arts Club, School Choir, and believe it or not I was part of a step team that was associated with MHC. I even participated in Pep Rally's as well. Now, of course, if there was something that I could not perform, I would need to sit out for the duration of that performance, but for the most part and most importantly, I was finally apart of a team that showed no judgment. Everyone did have to tryout, but no one was ever left out or dismissed from the organization. It was just all depending on that individual's strength and where they fit in as a group. Kind of like joining the choirs with the director having to figure out if you are an alto or a soprano based on your vocals. Metaphorically, the step team was based on nothing but a *coke and a smile*. Continuously, I volunteered and participated in majority events within the organizations I was a part of on a given day. I may not have been able to play sports activities, but I was still able to be part of a group, team, or organization of some sort. This meant a lot to me and also taught me to find my own individual identity regardless of my condition. This was definitely the beginning of "Arthritis and Me."

After my tenth grade year, I was forced to move in with my aunt Stephany, so that I could continue to get the education I needed to succeed in College. The high school I went to was a highly devoted educational school to prepare students for their college education. I continued my involvement in clubs and organizations, as well as continuing to try and keep my grades up to an A and B average. Although, I was involved in social organizations we still had criteria's that students needed to meet; just as if they were playing any other school related activities; the rules still applied. In order to be involved in any type of recreational activities, including, sports, clubs, and organization, it was required to keep your grades up at an A through C average. Since the level of education became challenging, there were times when it became difficult for me to meet those demands. When transferring from a low-grade school to a higher academically challenged institution; it became sort of a stretch for me to get caught up with the learning structure. My worst subject was English for the most part, but Math has always been my favorite. I understand English is my primary language, which is what my mother would always say, but that wasn't the hard part. It was the fact that I had to read these excerpts or sometimes a full chapter book and then answer questions about it with the understanding of what I had just read along with the tricky questions that were given. My learning is more effective hands-on than visual; so reading and answering questions can somewhat become a bit of a strain to understand, especially when it is regarding a topic that you could care less about. However, I did persist on maintaining my homework and any other assignments that were required of me, but sometimes I would become lazy and/or rush through my work to get it completed more quickly. Either way, I was still able to continue and manage to stay involved in my school's clubs and organizations, as well as participating in as many activities as possible.

I often spoke with my mother over the phone to update her on how I was doing with school and grades. My mother and majority family members have always babied me as if I was the same little girl who was just the happiest and sweetest thing but then grew up. I guess as you get older, sometimes it is hard to get out of that babying stage, because that is what you're still used to, as well as members of your family. I always felt that I had to come up with some kind of explanation to my mother on why I chose to do things or go a certain direction with my life; You always will continue to be that sweet pea and then you suddenly snap out of it, wake up and reassure yourself that you are not a little girl or boy anymore.

While going through the rest of my high school years my mother advised me to go to a community college to start off and get my associates degree; then after if I was up to it I could go to a 4-year college to further my education and receive my bachelor's degree. I cannot tell you how many times I have changed major. When figuring out what career I wanted for myself, it became difficult to choose from and I always thought I would pursue something in healthcare because majority of family members were in some type of health care field or getting advice on health. My aunt was an administrator at a nursing home, as well as me having an uncle who is married with a wonderful family and is an Occupational Therapist. After graduating high school, majors that I have chosen were being a Pediatrician, Nurse, Occupational Therapist, Physical Therapist, Social Worker, and even becoming a Teacher for elementary kids because Lord knows I wouldn't be able to find the strength to deal with any kind of adolescents. As you can see, I was pretty non-decisive.

CHAPTER 3

This is Me

Have you ever looked back at your past and said "how did I get here?" or see that you are not the same person that you used to be? Well, a little bit about myself. I was born in Queens, New York and was sent to live with my grandmother shortly after so that my mother could finish her Bachelor's degree in Nursing. I was brought up by my mother Elizabeth, sister Rebecca, and aunt Stephany with no sounds of my father at the time, until my teenage years. My mother was very much a single parent taking care of three children on her own and raised us very well if I might add.

Once my mother received her degree, she came to get me, my sister, and aunt from Miami, Florida and from there we moved to Houston, TX where we stayed in a two bedroom townhouse, and where I became diagnosed with Juvenile Rheumatoid Arthritis (JRA or RA). I have been diagnosed with also having Thalassemia Anemia, and Osteoporosis came along in my early 20's; due to having RA for so long. It is known that osteoporosis can cause bones to become fragile and easy to break; which I only thought occurred during old age, but I guess not. My mother and I, along with my aunt and sister then moved into a three-bedroom house where we had to transfer schools and my sister and aunt finally had graduated high school and went on with their lives shortly after.

My mother remarried and I had a baby brother named Will. Will currently graduated from high school in New York and is going off to college to further his education in Engineering. My aunt is currently a teacher and still resides in Houston, Texas. My sister currently owns her own business in nursing and lives in a smll town in Florida with her husband and 4 children; wonderful family. My mother is taking great care of my little brother and keeping him on the right path and showing him the definition of becoming successful for his own future; they are still currently living in New York and are doing great; speaking, "from the proud youngest daughter and second oldest sister." My family is originally from Kingston, Jamaica, but they all grew up in the U.S. My mother has been working her butt off to build a children's foundation in Jamaica to support young children and to gather clothes and food for people in need. I must say that she has a wonderful heart filled with the love and care for others, which is a beautiful thing. This is what makes the world a better place for people like her.

My mother has been a true inspiration to me along with my sister and aunt, who has a lot going for themselves and is doing very well with their lives, not to mention their careers. My father lives in Hartford, Conneticut followed by eight siblings that I know of. I grew up with my mother raising me through all my obstacles. Having someone who is rooting for you and making sure your condition is controlled is a wonderful feeling. My father does what he can to help me and I continue to appreciate him for what he does for me. I've never been a troubled kid. I was very shy but sweet and I have always kept to myself in school. I am very joke-ful and have an enthusiastic and outgoing attitude and just full of life.

Arthritis and Me

One thing I enjoy doing is giving back to others and volunteering at hospitals and nursing homes. I took care of my grandmother when she became sickly and had to put her in a nursing home. I was there every day to make sure I gave her a bath and did her hair before she passed. Everyone loved me and would come engage with the other residents and entertaining them by playing the piano in the lunch room. I took care of my grandfather while he was staying with my uncle and was diagnosed with Prostate cancer until he passed. Those were both my hearts and I miss them so much. My grandfather instilled the importance of having an education and being somebody important. I never have the time to visit my grandfather's grave site, because he is buried in Massachusetts, but I still celebrate his name one way or the other; whether it is on Facebook, Instagram, or something of that nature. However, every year me and my son go to visit my grandmother's grave on her birthday to place flowers and speak with her about what has been going on with me, my successes and problems that she has missed within the past year or so.

When it came to friends and other associates that I come into connect with. I was always the center of attention because of my wonderful personality. People enjoyed hanging out with me because of my sense of humor and my willingness to care for others and succeed in everything I do, just like my mother. Halfway through high school is when my mother, as well as my little brother moved back to New York due to some family issues that was going on around that time with a distant family member and also it was new start that I know my mother needed, since her pay in New York changed significantly for the better and with the cost of living it didn't make too much of a difference how much you got paid, but she was happier and that was all that mattered. My little brother received better opportunities for his education, as well as staying engaged and having a heart for playing football until he got hurt in the field, which put a stop to him getting any scholarships for college. Growing up, I was engaged in piano lessons and dance recitals. I have always loved the feel of music and entertainment; I loved being the star of the show. Everyone just thought I was the cutest thing, so why not act upon that standard. The only time I did not show an act of shyness was when I had to perform in front of an audience; only because I felt like I had no choice but to or be embarrassed. My biggest fear was making mistakes in front of a group of people when in the middle of a performance, which was not a good look. This was me growing up and enjoying my childhood years and life, regardless of my medical condition..

I have a wonderful family who cares and loves me and just want to see me succeed in life. I never been sneaky or tried to hide anything from my mother unless it had to do with my grades; who hasn't? Whenever I received my report card, I would hope for my grades to be at an A and B average or I was definitely in trouble. I used to forge my mother signatures if I knew my grade did not meet up to her standards. I rarely got any whoopings from my mother because she would be sensitive to my condition of having arthritis. If I did get a whooping, best believe my grade had to have been horrible, at least a D or below and sometimes a C; depending on what that C was for, but that was very seldom. My mother did not play those games, especially when it came to her kid's education.

I always stayed involved in school, since I was not able to play in any sports or other extracurricular activities because of the stress to my joints. My favorite sport that I wanted to play in high school was soccer, which was not possible due to the fact that a lot of running was involved and I did not want to make the mistake in having an accidental fall and possibly being hospitalized. At the age of 16, my first job was at a pizza place and after, I had worked inside a movie theatre located behind the snack bar. My mother paid for me to go to driving school, so that I could get my driver's license, which is how I got my first car that was given to me by my uncle, who also took part in helping my mother raise me to be the person I am today.

CHAPTER 4

College Life

After graduating high school, I knew that whatever decision I made as my career goal; I knew I wanted to go away for college and check out the experience of being on my own with no adult supervision and so that I was able to see what else was out there and explore other options. This was finally my chance to become independent and finding my true self in seeing what the world was all about while meeting new people. Before my graduation, while still living with my aunt Stephany and her two kids, I had applied at quite a few colleges in-state and out-of-state to speed up my *acceptance* from universities a lot quicker and paying for application fees and sending any transcripts that needed to be sent. Couple of weeks later, I received a congratulations letter from Lamar University, located in Beaumont, TX, which was only an hour in a half away and that I needed to call and set up an appointment for a visit to tour the school. I was so excited, that I told my mother about my acceptance and how I will finally be able to go away and my aunt will be able to have the house all to herself.

My mother always offered me advice on what she thought was best for me, but mostly I made my own decisions. I can admit that I was in fact a stubborn child, but only I could try to figure out what the big bad world was all about and learn from my mistakes. I was always small minded and never looked at the bigger picture of things. I would rush into everything, and we all know when you rush into something, it never tends to work out the way you want to. My mother always instilled in my heart that, "there are consequences to your actions." I believed that; but, never sure of what that had to do with me since I was the type who rarely did anything wrong and would try my best to live up to any of my mother's rules in our household. All I could think to myself is that I am a good girl and always have been and always will be, regardless of what others thought about me. I tried to stay out of one's business and remain the good girl I was. I didn't dare think about having sex, sneaking boys in the house, or even thinking about getting pregnant; so what actions did I have to pursue? Nothing, but an education for myself, and picking up a few skills along the way. I will say, if you are the type that is easily influenced by your peers, then knowing that there are consequences to your action, would be the best advice for you. Trust, It can happen. I could honestly say I wish I had listened to my mother a long time ago and maybe things would go a little more productive than what I had planned.

Below is a letter that I had written to my mother in **February 2004** when I was eighteen years old with the thought of having it all figured out:

February 2004

Dear mom,

"I just wanted to tell you that I love you and I always will. Now that I am about to graduate high school and go off to college. I just want you to know that you no longer have to worry so much about me. I think it is time for me to explore the real world and let me find out for myself what life is all about. You have always been there for me with no help from my father. You seen me take my first walk, the first time I used the potty, my first job, and most importantly when I became diagnosed with Juvenile Rheumatoid Arthritis and now College. Even when my doctor told me that I would be in a wheelchair at the age of 15; look at me now still standing and that is all because of you. I want you to understand that I am not a little girl anymore and I am nothing like Stephany and Rebecca. I have not had sex or gotten pregnant. I never had AID's or an STD. I am officially clean. I have continued to maintain my grades at an A and B average. I understand that I do have arthritis and that is probably what have you worried the most. But, I believe that I can fight and live on my own with no problems. **THAT DOESN'T MEAN THAT I DON'T WANT YOU IN MY LIFE!** I never want you to give up on me or forget about me. I still want you in my life and to continue to stay by my side whenever I need you! Anyways mom I just want you to know that you are always in my heart and do hope you like this card from me to you and to continue to pray for me and ask God to keep me safe! I LOVE YOU AND MISS YOU!"

Love You Always,
Monique Shante Mckenzie aka Mona

Class of 2004

This was me; this is what I have always kept in my heart and still do. I was a believer and I knew that I could make a difference in my path and better myself to be someone important. My issue was being distracted and being influenced by the wrong people. I had continued staying with my aunt Stephany until I graduated high school and then went off to Lamar University, where I saw "freedom." Bad idea!

I never thought of my life taking a full turn on me as it did. I was meeting new and different people that I never think existed and involving myself in various activities to keep me occupied while away from home. I have seen others with recreational drugs that I was very curious about and just to see how it would feel. I had always been easily influenced as a young child entering the adult stage. As I was supposed to be attending class at Lamar University, after some weeks had passed I started playing hooky and hanging out with these low-grade men that were around my age group, along with attending night clubs, Frat parties, and whatever consisted of "fun" for college level students on or off campus. This was not me, but an experience of a whole other lifestyle that I was never introduced to. After a few months of meeting and getting to know other students on campus and checking out the city of Beaumont off campus, I started dating the wrong type of men and further on became pregnant with someone who insisted on me having an abortion because he already had two kids and was not ready for another. This was not an option and had caused me to have to deal with the entire nine months pregnancy alone, including going to the doctor's office for checkups alone, being cheated on, and being treated unfairly, and poorly. I drove a '96' Black Volvo 850 that he wrecked and was stuck driving a "hooptie" with no a/c.

Later, my baby's father and I decided to try the "family thing" and get our own place, which did not seem to work either, because I was treated disrespectfully and I needed to come to the realization that he was not going to change his careless ways. It's funny how someone can say they care about you one minute and turn around, then stab you in the back the next, only because "responsibility" rose up in the air. It was time to fend for myself and move back in with my aunt Stephany until my baby came. My aunt helped me get through everything and was there every step of the way with the birth of my baby Christian. If it wasn't for her ain't no telling where I would be. Christian came into this world with no father, but my job is to make sure that he always know who was there from day one.

CHAPTER 5

Life's Existence

Through everything that I had experienced in life, something great came from it. I have a wonderful, intelligent, and handsome son that I would not trade the world for. After I had Christian, I stayed with my aunt for about a month and moved off to go live with my sister Rebecca and my two nieces in Massachusetts. The plan was to go to work and finish college with the support and help from Rebecca. I was able to find work and fill out the application to go back to college. I needed to remain focused so that I may finally graduate to receive my Bachelor's degree.

I was working for Charter Cable Company; which was a call center where I was making $10.00 an hour, helping clients sign up for cable and internet service. My son was taken care of at an in-home childcare center, whom my sister knew and trusted. At that moment, I was breastfeeding Christian which was a major challenge due to the fact I had to continuously pump my breast so that Christian received all the proper nutrients and because he loved the breast milk better than formula or he would not make any attempts to drink it. He was very stubborn. While at work, I could not tell you the amount of accidents and clothes I had to change because my breast would leak for the eight hours of being at work and unfortunately breast pads weren't no help; it was almost like being on your menstrual cycle. I had to stop taking my medicine throughout my entire pregnancy and for the first three months after Christian was born so that I could remain breastfeeding Christian. Normally, you had to breastfeed for at least a minimum of six months, but I also needed to maintain my health of arthritis so that I could contain a productive lifestyle for my child and I. Moreover, I was not able to go any longer in breastfeeding Christian, because I had to get back on my meds and so that my joints did not possibly become inflamed.

It was such a wonderful experience becoming a mother for the first time and I had plenty of emotional suppresses because I was seeing the stress of taking care of a child and being a single mother with no help from the father himself. I continued to stay with my sister for about a month or so, but because I was so used to my environment in Houston, Tx, I became uncomfortable with my living situation. In Houston, everything is more spaced out and slower, and unlike up North, Houston didn't seem so bad as far as the weather went. Living in the Northern part of the U.S., the people and places were fast paced and the weather was much colder around the snowy season. I knew that I would be better off living in Houston for the sake of my condition. When the weather is cold my joints tend to get stiff and swollen and I can barely walk at times, especially early mornings when I wake up. This caused me to have to take pain killers, warm baths or showers to relax my joints and get me through the day moving and cruising.

When finally coming to the realization that Houston was the best option for the sake of me, my health, and the well-being of Christian who can grow to have a mother who is physically and mentally able to interact with him. I was able to move back with aunt Stephany up until my child turned a little after one-year-old and get a job working at Wal-mart in Tomball, Tx. My childhood best friend Chamille, with Christian and me, had come to a decision to become roommates so that we could save money and help each other pay rent and utilities for our new apartment. My aunt suggested that it was a good idea so that we could split the rent and help each other as much as possible, which we agreed was the smart thing to do. While Chamille, Christian, and I were planning the move from my aunt Stephany's house and still maintaining my job at Wal-mart, our first move as young adults in our own place was a success. Everything was working out perfectly and I was finally living the life and doing everything I needed to do to keep my child in a safe, loving environment. The apartment wasn't too bad and had everything we needed to be comfortable. Chamille was wonderful and sometimes she could be a little too much at times and very pushy; all because she loved everything to go her way. What made us so different was that I was a single mother and she had no children. Chamille was free spirited and wanted to hang out and just have fun and she could do that. Of course, there is nothing wrong with wanting to have a great time, but I had other priorities that required much more attention. This was the start of my maturity level progressing to be the perfect role model for my son.

Chamille and I were like sisters, we grew up in the same neighborhood and came from the same tracks. We both came from cultural backgrounds which made us understand each other even better, because of the type of parents we were raised by. Meanwhile, Chamille and I lived in the two bedroom apartment together with little Christian and had very interesting neighbors who lived only a few doors down from us. With being wrapped up in motherhood, sometimes I would lose sight of that and would hang out with my neighbors who had nothing going for themselves at the time. My neighbors also had kids that behaved badly and would use all kinds of profanity. This is the group that I would surround my child and I with. I started becoming so in-tuned with my neighbors that they even turned me against my own best friend. I was the type of person that was a follower instead of a person who led by example. I admit that I was the blame for engaging myself with such horrible people.

Chamille and I stayed in the apartment for a couple of months until we got into a huge brawl. This happened because my neighbors were envious of Chamille because of her body structure and would go out for her morning workouts without trying to drive any attention to anyone and stayed to herself. Chamille never felt the need to speak with the neighbors, so to them they felt as if she was just being stuck up and insubordinate towards them; this was not the case. Just like me she was not used to that type of environment, but she was more of a leader than a follower, unlike me. Chamille and I had got into some issues because I started listening and becoming drawn into my neighbor's foolish habits and ways. At times, I thought that Chamille sometimes would try to take over my life by telling me what to do and how to do it. My mind was so messed up at the time, that I planned to move out without giving Chamille any type of notice and leaving her stuck with the rent and utilities to settle by herself. When it came time for Christian and I to finally move out, two of my neighbors including their child who was only about 11 years old had set Chamille up because they were so full of resentment towards someone that never spoke two words to them. I allowed this to happen, but I never meant for it to go down that way and Chamille figured that I set the whole thing up so these girls could jump on her. Chamille called her cousin to get involved and she came by quick as lightning to make an attempt to fight me. I jumped in my car while my child was with me and sped off so they couldn't find me and know where I had moved to. Chamille's cousin texted threatening and abusive languages were thrown at me causing me to get the police involved for harassment. I started having shortness of breath and had to call my sister about what happened. I was so embarrassed by the situation that I told my sister what she needed to hear. My sister forced me to call them on three-way and stated to them, "If you so touch one hair on my sister's head, I will take the next flight out there and you will have me to deal with." My sister, Rebecca was not the one to play with when she was upset and was the type to stick to her every word, especially when it came to her family. I can't say stuff got any better but it was a start and this time, it was just Christian and I. Chamille and I stopped being friends for three years. It took time to recover those wounds that were never meant to happen and of course, Chamille was curious to know if I had anything to do with why these girls decided to jump on her. I explained to her that it was never my intentions, period. After months of living with Chamille, I did feel some type of way, as if she was trying to take control of my life. I know that she is looking out for my well-being, but she needed to allow me to make my own decisions that I knew were the right ones for my child and I. We are good friends now and have made the choice to forgive one another and forget the past. This occurred after finally finding one another on Myspace three years later and making amends.

Later, I had moved into my new apartment that was near Northwest Houston. I had got fired from Wal-mart because I had a little run in with my manager who had a discrimination issue and was showing favoritism towards certain employees, and was not being equal to all employees and I got my feelings involved and started calling in more often. I started working at a call center for bestbuy.com; where customers called in to order products and services throughout the call center. The items were ordered for them over the phone only if they were experiencing difficulties with their own computers, or were not computer savvy and needed some assistance in placing their orders. I was top seller every quarter, won awards and quarterly bonuses every time for my hard work and accomplishments. Working at a stable job has always been a challenge for me. I wore myself out so easily to the point where I did not feel like working or doing anything for that matter, but I had to for the sake of Christian and our apartment. Responsibilities started to become more and more real as Christian got older and my options for childcare was exclusive. It was time to enroll my baby in daycare to remain working so that I could provide for him and to ensure the bills got paid. My aunt Stephany at time was a helping hand for keeping Christian on the weekends and holidays, if I had to work. If she was not available, Christian would spend some nights with my Godmother, Shirley or at his Godparent's house.

Later, things started to become difficult and I would still able to help others when I barely could help myself; but, I always kept the faith to know that God had something greater and beneficial for me in the near future. I was always strong and prepared for whatever came my way and if someone needed something, I would always ask myself "what would Jesus do?" Selfishness is the one characteristic that I did not have. A few weeks later, I get a phone call from my cousin to move in with me because he was having family issues at home in Florida. I was happy at the time to have him stay with us and keep Christian and I company. This was his last year of high school, so I had to enroll him in school as his guardian so he could complete 12th grade and get his high school diploma. When he moved everything was fine until he started to invite personal friends over to spend the night. At one point I was okay with it, but then it had began to get out of hand. I could not handle his careless manner one bit. When it came to my child, my son, Christian, it is my job to make sure I protect him and what he see going on in my household. I stayed in the apartment for only about three months until I got evicted due to non-payment of rent. Again, I had to find a new place for my child and I to live and had to inform my cousin that we were moving out and going to the North side of Houston and he was more than welcome to come along; he chose to go along a different path, in which I was relieved because I was never too fond of his choice in friends. It was difficult to share the news with him because it was my *big mouth* that allowed him to come to Texas in the first place. My cousin never respected my authority and chose to do what he wanted, so him finding some place else to stay was fine by me. My cousin and I had our moments where we did not see eye to eye and at times would be best of friends. When we did not get along, it had a certain effect on my two-year-old child and I was not going for that. I take full responsibilities for the decisions that I have made and it is my job as an individual and as someone's mother, to lead by example.

CHAPTER 6

My Hardships

Once again, I was evicted from the apartment that I was living in on the North side and I could feel my stress building up and joints progressively getting more and more stiff and achy. I had no place to live at this time and was welcome to my cousin's house for Christian and I to spend the night because she already had too many people living there. I had no choice but to ask my aunt Stephany if it was ok for Christian and I to stay for a few weeks until I could finally get back on my feet. My aunt resided in a two-bedroom apartment for money-saving purposes, and had a roommate that was also contributing to the household; so you can imagine how cramped we were along with her two boys that would come over on the weekends. Christian was only about a year old and my aunt could only give us a week to stay at there. The very next day she informed us that we could not stay because the house was too crowded, not to mention she had a roommate who was probably uncomfortable with the living arrangement. This was understood but I did not know what else to do or where else I could possibly go with Christian with me, this became very difficult and frustrating. This was another turning point in my life that I had to experience on my own. I just needed a little assistance to get back on my feet. I was very understanding and if that is how it needed to be; well, leaving was not a problem. It was just trying to get myself together with a baby was very difficult to do, but I guess I didn't have much of a choice but to figure other alternatives.

As I left my aunt Stephany's apartment, I sat in my car thinking of my next move. Stephany was really my last to nothing hope, besides my Godmother that I know would have welcomed us with open arms; but, I didn't want to bother her with any of my problems or even ask anyone else for anything anymore just to be disappointed again. While in deep thought and with my mind going a million miles per minute, about what my next move should be and what place could we lay our head. In the year 2007, MySpace was popular before Facebook. These were social media sites where you meet new people in your area and who would find an interest in someone and vice-versa. This guy that I continued to message, he invited me to his townhome on the Southwest side of Houston and with me explaining my current situation, he insisted for Christian and I to stay with him for a few days. I had to put my pride to the side and contact my baby's father sister in Beaumont, who I knew was able to welcome us with open arms and would not want her own nephew out on the street. My pride was very high to the extreme, I did not like to involve my family in any of my problems, especially my mother. I didn't want to worry anyone and start hearing them make a decision that they figured was right for me. I called his sister and informed her of my current situation, she said that it was okay for us to stay with her until I was able to get back on my feet. Thankfully, I had my tax refund coming right around the corner, so once I received that, I knew that I was going to be able to get everything together and find my own apartment and job. I had a plan just no money at the time. It was just a matter of waiting for it to be direct deposited into my bank account.

Once received my income tax refund, I had asked my baby father's oldest sister if it was okay for Christian to stay with her until I was able to get myself together and I would come back for him as soon as everything was stable; she agreed. My income tax was approximately around $2,500, so I had to make sure I budgeted my expenses correctly. This was enough to get back on track and bring my baby back home. As I am driving back to Houston, I am thinking about what my game plan is going to be. What am I going to do when I get there? Where are we going to stay? I made a few calls to see where I could lay my head at until I was able to find a job and a place to live. The first person I called was my previous college buddy Erica who resided outside the city limits, at about 45 minutes away outside of Houston. Erica allowed me to stay with her for a day at her mother's home and we would go out to find a hotel in Houston to where I can be comfortable at and apply for some jobs at the same time. After my stay in the hotel and paying for it day by day, Erica spent quite a few nights with me in the hotels and continued to stay near me every step of the way, for at least a couple of weeks or until she figured it was time for her to go back home. I appreciated Erica for being with me through my rough times and doing what she could.

Sometimes I had thoughts of giving up, but all I could think of was I miss my baby Christian and I needed to bring him back home as soon as possible. My cousin who Christian and I had spent the night with, she contacted m4e and come to find out she was not doing so well herself. I decided to meet up with her at her hotel and see how she was holding up. It had been about six months or more since I seen her and it was kind of a relief seeing someone that was also going through the same exact struggle and trying to get by. This was a way for us to help each other and work together to get back on both our feet.

My cousin and I had begun to search for an apartment and I had finally found a new job working at another call center, similar to an office setting structure. It didn't matter what kind of job it was as long as I had money coming in and it was consistent. I managed to get an apartment quickly after I received a few paychecks so that I could hurry to go back to Beaumont and pick up Christian. Coincidentally, my cousin had also signed up for the same apartment complex. Later, I ran into a former guy friend that was like a father to Christian and a great person to hang with, he just didn't have no moral values what-so-ever, but sad to say, I developed strong feelings for him before he gained any for me. He and I both kept a job and was residing with his sister around this time and would occasionally spend the night at my place. We even thought it made sense to become roommates and go half on the rent for the apartment. Although we made this agreement, when it came to the next months rent, he was nowhere to be found and wouldn't come back to the apartment within a week or two. He spent most of the nights hanging out with his friends doing God knows what.

Nevertheless, he always made it understood that he was a free man, who was not interested in being in a committed relationship. I would occasionally ask him to be my boyfriend since we had major feelings for each other. It took us a little over two years before he came to the decision to want to settle down and build something with me. This was me, this was all me! I wanted a family, I wanted to be loved, I wanted to be cherished, and most of all I wanted to be wanted…to sum it all up…A FUTURE! I tried very hard to get to where I wanted to be to be where I am now. Men could see my ambitious potential, but never looked towards the advantage. This guy had potential, or that I thought; but, something was always holding him back. I realized shortly after that you cannot make a man have that passion and love for what you are looking for, they have to be ready and willing, only because sometimes what you want may not be the same as what they want, and it's okay! I realized this when it became too late. I went through a five-year relationship with this man and within those five years, it was wasted with lies, deceit, pain, distrust, and infidelity.

Due to all this, I promised to no longer give away my heart to the next person, who may actually be the right person, but with everything I have been through it came to a point where I did not know how to open my heart again to someone new. I stopped longing for something that I believed I couldn't or will never receive. My focus was placed towards other things that a man wish he could've had and run with that without looking back at the past. This was not over one relationship alone that messed me up and had blocked my mindset. I had to change the game up because the way my personal life and relationships were going; it was time for a transition. I am a fighter and if one way don't work, my position was showing others who found my intelligence lacking that I didn't need them in my life and that I was better off in a positive standpoint and did not want nothing to do with any sort of negativity that distracted or try to influence any decisions I made for the future. Everything that I have spoken of or stated to a man and what my dreams are is now coming true and they are now and forever the last ones standing while I have the last laugh! This is about me, what I have learned, what I have conquered, and what I will continue to accomplish. My destiny is waiting and it is still more to come.

CHAPTER 7

Good Relationship or NOT!

Dealing with arthritis was and still can be difficult when dealing with relationships. What do a lot of us woman dream about when it comes to a stable relationship? I can't speak for everyone, but I have always wanted to live that happily ever after life. The kinds of life where you get married, start a family, and live your life in a happy home. I see this everyday where people are so in love and holding hands, which just makes me sick to my intestines. This is not something I like to elaborate too much on, but it is the way of life and describes how most females who are looking forward to success and doesn't want to just have a career to look forward to with no one to share it with.

The majority of my relationships never seemed to work out because of my choice in men and sometimes sexual pleasures also played a factor when being intimate. I always chose the men who had nothing going for themselves, no jobs or minimal pay, and definitely no ambition to succeed in life and was just comfortable with the way life was. The kind of guys at the time that matched my preference was someone who protects, who was tall, muscular, dark-skinned, and had a future going for them. It seemed difficult to find the one who wanted to settle down with one person and build a future together. I guess in this day and age somehow I just had no luck in finding Mr. Right.

Being with a guy for almost eight years in total around the year 2007; the relationship showed nothing proceeding to a further commitment that would lead to a promising future. I was looking for a commitment between my partner and I or a relationship that would lead up to us being committed and building that happily ever after-ending that I have always wanted. I was very determined. I had my own job as a Customer Service Representative at a loan company through another childhood friend that I ran into off of Myspace in 2005. Later, I received a promotion as an assistant manager and further was promoted to a store manager three years of being with the company. I went through hoops to get there and maintain that status, so if I ever became laid off or even quit, then I would forever be able to continue searching for additional jobs in that position due to my experience and of course able to get a well-deserved salary. I was a shooter for higher, never low, and never turning back to a $9.00 per hour job. The loan company that I used to work for brought about my expertise that I could use in today's world. My paychecks were magnificent. I have never seen a paycheck that had four figures. I received all this because of my drive to learn and succeed in everything that I could get my hands on.

My mother gave me her old house for Christian and I to live. The house was built in 1981 and needed a lot of work too. Windows needed to be replaced, walls needed to be painted, carpets needed to be replaced, the roof needed to be replaced, I mean this whole place needed just a whole makeover. The great thing about the house is that you could remodel it up to your standards. I was only responsible for paying the $500.00 towards the mortgage payment. Each year during income tax season, I would repair anything major in the house, so that Christian and I would be comfortable and not to mention the guy I was dating at that time wouldn't offer any assistant to help with the house as it needed work. This was all me that rejuvenated the house and even did all the labor on my own such as painting the living room, and bedrooms etc, so that the house could have a new home feeling. All this took a lot of hard work and dedication, but someone had to do it. Having a man's help, especially ones I dated was not an option. Another thing about me, I was never the type to ask for any help; I had pride. If someone is doing hard work, then I know common sense should tell you to offer your services and not lay back and watching television; but, who am I to judge! Girl code don't judge me.

CHAPTER 8

Turning Point
(Reunited In Peace)
As Brooklyn remain in Heaven

September 16, 2014 ended, with my favorite cousin, William. We shared something special that was unbreakable and that no one person could damage the relationship that we had. In completion to our delicious Sunday dinner September 14th, all three of us around the dinner table laughing and cracking jokes. The moment I will never forget. I cannot tell you the last time, we shared this bond; been awhile, since we were kids! This was my cousin, my brother, my family, why he had to do this? This was unfair to Christian, especially. Was there anything I could have done to prevent this from happening? I should've came with him. I blamed myself!!! He was nervous as I was for his final court date. The trouble he caused and could not get back, changed his life. 15 to 25 years away for sentencing scared him and made him lose all hope. I prayed and kept the faith for a miracle to take place. William woke up before Christian and I without a trace of seeing or speaking to let us know he was leaving for court. I heard the sound of the door slamming at six in the morning and noticed that he's never left this early to catch the bus to downtown. He was not scheduled to appear in court for the next four hours. William informed me the day before that I would hear from his lawyer what the final ruling would be, only because he did not want me to know what he was up to.

In 2013, William, who was known as *Brooklyn*, we were very close, but he fell into a lot of trouble over a current situation that became difficult for him to resolve on his own. After being freed, I made the promise to his father; my uncle, that I would be able to watch over him and make sure that he stayed committed to arriving to court on time. William was forced to reside with me until the decision on his sentence was made. He was very smart and had a lot of potential in him to become someone important, even though the choices he made now became in effect with his future upcomings. I was very disappointed with the decision that he had made to go all the way center-left field in his role that affected him and his family's life.

William and I were very tight; we were like brothers and sisters, Batman and Robin, Fred and Barney from the *Flinstones*; we understood each other. We would offer each other advice of female and male characteristics to understand the reason behind their persona, especially, when it came to our involved relationships. While getting information from William about guys I have dated in the past, he could not understand their way of thinking and the things they did or didn't do. William just could not make out the reason for my careless choices for some reason, especially the ex that I was in a five-year relationship with. William was like my 24-hour shadow, outside looking in and seeing it all, while currently staying with us. There was even times he had to protect me from my ex because he wouldn't leave my house, which suffered into a huge brawl between them, causing cops to become involved.

William's stay with us reminded me of when we were little, the conversations that we had were deep. We held discussions about life accomplishments for the near future. I would share with William my dreams and he would share with me his. We talked about everything. One out of many conversations were about my passion for dancing and singing, but William and I knew that due to my limitations of the arthritis I had to face the reality that I may not be able to go that direction in my career. The next best thing was becoming an event planner. I enjoyed the exhilaration of planning events for family and friends, and creating custom designs such as, business cards, post cards, invitations, flyers, brochures, and so forth, so why not turn that into a career. I may not be singer or a dancer in the future, but it's still in the entertainment field. William and I understood each other and he showed mutual support for my dreams and would encourage me to go for it. We were thinkers and always had wonderful ideas to share with one another. I loved my cousin to death; we were like Ben and Jerry. Ha, Ha! All smiles on this end!

William was my cousin, my hero, the protector of the household, and my brother over all things; He was there for me and I was there for him. While he continued staying with Christian and I, he would contribute around the house and assist Christian with his homework when he came home from school. It was a relief having an actual man around the house, while I was at work, and knowing that everything was taken care of at home. Despite his behavior, he was someone I could count on. I instilled the power of keeping his head up and remain thinking positive, and that he always had a home with us. He never thought he had a place in my heart before he committed his crime, because of the fact that we had lost touch and we both were too busy with our separate lives. What he did was un-thought of and he regrets every bit of it. William stayed becoming depressed and I knew I had to make sure that his mindset didn't shut down and give up hope, because of his inappropriate act. I was the type that could talk anyone out of anything, especially him, but at the same time he was grown, an adult, only 24 years of age and I knew he needed some reassurance. He needed help him and my uncle knew that I was the only person that could get through to him most of the time, but at the end of the day, he had his own mind and personal opinions about certain things. I am a firm believer that God put people in our lives for a reason and it was his time. He was just in need of family support.

During the time that William stayed with us, Christian started to look up to him as the brother he never had. I knew William enjoyed the fact that Christian looked up to him and was willing to make sure he influences Christian in a positive way. I know the hurt Christian will have once he finds out what William had done.

It's the afternoon; I did not receive a call from William or his attorney. I went ahead and called his lawyer's office and was forwarded to the voice message. Two hours passed and I finally received a call back from William's attorney. William didn't show up on time for court and he was supposed to actually appear September 15th, yesterday. How was it possible for William to miss court on the day he was supposed to go to court? Hmmm… The date was scheduled for September 15th and not the 16th to go to the hearing. William lied to me. The lawyer suggested to me that if I hear from him that the best thing for him to do was to go ahead and turn himself in. I told the lawyer that I would let him know as soon as I heard from him and then slowly hung up the phone with the sudden thoughts in my head as to what was going on and where could my cousin be if he isn't in court. Within two minutes, a best friend of mine named, Precious was with me at the time driving from the gas station and about to enter incoming traffic when suddenly the lawyer called back with disturbing news.

The first thing the lawyer said, "It may be best to sit down." This wasn't sounding too good. I asked the attorney, "Why? What's wrong?" He stated that he had received a call from the Houston Police Department (HPD) that my cousin was found dead on the third floor building on Main St. where the courthouse was taken place. I screamed and tears started drifting down my face in no time, like a waterfall. I couldn't believe what I was hearing. I was trembling and could no longer get my words out. I felt a panic attack leaving out the store and I had to stop before I entered traffic. My vision became blurry, due to the high amount of tears. Never in my life did I suspect something like this would ever happen to me, to my cousin, "oh my God, Please help me!" How do I even begun to explain this to my son, to the family, more importantly, my uncle, and William's father, who was currently in Jamaica. After hearing the news and the lawyer telling me how sorry he was for my loss. I lost it! With Precious in the passenger seat and watching me shed my tears, was curious to know what I found out, and knew that it couldn't have been good. She took the phone when she seen me no longer being able to speak with the attorney. I laid on the steering wheel still screaming and crying and could not control the movement of my hands while behind the wheel of my car. Precious had spoken with the lawyer briefly to find out what happened and were they certain that it was him. The lawyer confirmed that the police did ID him and it was in fact William Crimson Mckinley as shown on his Identification card along with his tablet that he took with him everywhere he went. My heart dropped and again I could barely breathe; this time my breaths became shorter and shorter and I went into panic attack mode. "Nooooooooo!" While still bawling out of control.

After informing family members about William's death, I called into work and told my manager that I was not able to come in and she could tell by the sound of my voice and heavy breathing that something tragic must've happened. I missed out on days of work, which turned into weeks, and then I just went ahead and put in my two weeks' notice. I fell into a deep depression leading up to William's Memorial service that I volunteered to put together with the help from a few family members. I gained 30 pounds to my average weight causing me to weight over 200 pounds. I never once believed I could get that big until I observed certain photos leading up to the service and my mother and sister noticing the excessive amount of weight that I put on. I had a pink eye that I did not know where on earth it came from and I believed it to be from crying heavily. While coming into work and trying to pull my feelings together, I was showing signs of panic attacks and depression. If my manager left the store to go run an errand or went on lunch break, I would start breaking out in tears and chill bumps would appear on my skin. It was a proven fact that I was not able to be by myself and these symptoms continued happening for at least a month. Christian had to sleep with me in my room to keep me company and I wasn't stable enough to continue working. My mindset was totally off and I was not able to keep my focus. I was $200.00 short in my cash drawer from work because I lost all my concentration. I knew I couldn't go on with this job; I wanted to just walk out at one point and not look back. My manager was a kind hearted woman and she made certain that I was okay and she did her best to help me get through resigning my position as an assistant manager. The district manager was understanding and concerned about me as well, but she approved my resignation to leave in one week instead of two, although she tried her best to get me to stay with the company.

When my grandparents passed, I never felt so lost or out of place, as I did with my cousin. I wish he seen how much his friends and family really loved him and just give us a chance to help him with his situation. I was lucky that the arthritis didn't flare-up because of this tragic experience with losing my cousin. With the excess weight gain and emotions, and having an infection in the eye, I came out of this situation very strong. It even came down to me having to involve this amazing motivational speaker from the suicide hotline, Barbara, who was honored to speak at the memorial to reach out to everyone, especially young adults. Before the memorial took place, Barbara helped me through everything and gave me one-on-one advice that started to make sense. The best advice she could ever give was to allow myself to get it all out and once I finally do, get back on track and continue following my dreams. She was right! I had to stop drowning myself in self-pity, because this was William's choice to do this and there was no possible way I could have stopped him, even if I tried.

For William, my best friend, my brother, my cousin, and my love who will never be forgotten---Rest in Peace!

CHAPTER 9

Becoming an Aspiration to Be an Inspiration

Out with the old and in with the new! All I can say is I have made it through the rain, storm, and hail. I have had my share of partying, drinking, smoking, and walking through dead end relationships. I have suffered the lost of my two dearest cousins; one who lived in New York and passed away by a drunk driver two years ago, who served in the military and one through suicide a year ago and resided with me at the time. I have hung out with the wrong group of people and associated myself with wrongful thinking. Through it all, I never lost sight of my duties as an individual with an illness, or the upcomings of being a single mother, who is continually striving for greatness.

Anyone who knew me knew my struggles, as well as my strengths. My strengths overcame the struggles that I have been through regardless of any bad decisions I made. As I look back, I begin to realize that everything is a lesson learned, leading to a positive gain. I had to go through different aspects in my life to prepare me for the future so that I could grow as a determined individual. Spiritually now, I have matured and grown into a woman who knows where she's been and knows where she is going and what's expected out of life for herself and child. I am honored to say that I have been an inspiration to plenty of individuals in my life, and have noticed the ins and outs of my efforts to get to where I am now and will be in the future. A very close friend of mine, who I still hang around with from time to time and has seen and even been part of my rough patches in life and is currently in College to get her degree in Real Estate. Speaking of college; here is a paper she wrote in one of her classes that she wrote about *yours truly:*

My Inspirational Story

"When life hands you lemons, you make lemonade. Funny, Funny, Lemonade" http://www.likazing.com/bad-situation/. I chose to write a story about my best friend; Monica Mckinley whom I've known for 7 years. This woman has had Rheumatoid Arthritis since the age of 6 years old; she has been through so much in her life and still continues to walk with her chin held high. Monica is a single mother, who has dealt with bad relationships, promotional jobs, and with the honor of being mother and father to her son. I truly look up to her, because although Monica has experienced a difficult life on managing on her own two feet with her son by her side. Nevertheless, she refuses to lose herself in the midst of the storm.

Monica once more, has had Rheumatoid Arthritis since the age of six years old. She was told by her Rheumatologist, that she would be in a wheelchair and barely able to move at the age of fifteen. Next month, this beautiful, strong willed and young lady will be thirty and continues moving as if nothing and no one can bring her down. Monica, growing up has faced multiple hardships; especially, during her school years. She has faced being made fun of from middle to high school, because of her weight and diagnosis. Monica never allowed anything considered stupidity get in her way because of childish behaviors from other students. This woman has joined and volunteered with numerous clubs and organizations while in high school to continue promoting a dynamic lifestyle; since sports involved too much movement than she could bare. When having Rheumatoid Arthritis, studies show that it limits your ability to engage in certain activities, due to not enough cartilage between her joints to allow her to be flexible like other kids. Growing up, Monica states that she fell into depression off and on all the way, up to 21 years of age; at that time, she then became more accepting to her condition.

I have observed Monica going through tough, serious relationships with men and being the type of person that she is: Kind, loving, loyal, smart, and very creative. Guys tend to take her kindness for weakness; and continue to make her a believer that she can actually have the family that she has always wanted. She is the type of person that will give you her shirt off her back to stay dry, her jacket to stay warm, and her last dime if she has it. All her experiences that had occurred in her past life, it did not budge to let her down. As a matter of fact, it only made her stronger as a person, as well as a single parent.

Monica has always kept a job to support her and her son. Arthritis in her means, can be stressful when having to go to work, pay for daycare, purchase needed goods, and pay bills with no sound-help from her son's father. She proclaims, "I have been through rough roads; but what keeps me going is there is someone else in this world that is far worse than me, so who am I to complain. It's not that bad," she continued. Monica states that she is grateful to have a son that keeps her on her toes and is so full of life. Watching Monica is like watching a television show on *Oprah*; so full of *love* and *inspirational* acts towards a promising future for her and her son.

In conclusion, I could continue to go on and on about my best friend's lifestyle forever; but this is just to show others that no matter what you are going through in life, always continue to push harder. Everything you go through in life is a *test* to prove how strong you are to get through it. If you allow life to knock you down, you will then continue to stay down; but, if you continue to push yourselves as well as others, you will then succeed and be ready for the next level to your own promising future. My bestie, Monica Mckinley is a clear example of inspirational success. I am writing my inspirational story, in who I look up to and who I want to be as strong as. This shows a situation that Monica thought was dreadful, but ended up turning out to be a great thing. She has come a long way and I hope that everyone will see this story as being one of their personal favorites.

-Franchesca Jones-
(aka Caress)

I felt so honored to be the one to also inspire her to go a different direction with her own life. Caress has been doing great and I just want to share how proud I am of her and her accomplishments.

It feels good to know people can see me as this person, an idol who has a purpose and believe me I do have a purpose when it comes to my life and the life of my child. I see others just like me who are single mothers and continue to fall down the wrong path and live this free lifestyle as if they have no responsibilities. I guess a lot of my strong-willed personality comes from the way I was raised. My mother at times would even be bothered by the fact of me having so much pride and independence in all that I do. I have been so close to just being homeless and I never allowed that to stop me with my powerful continuance of busting my butt for the sake of my child. I continue to inspire young girls to be the best that they can be and don't fall into the traps of a man with no ambition whatsoever.

As Steve Harvey would say, "men are hunters" don't go looking for a man because it may not be the one God placed in your life. I have learned that God puts people in your life for a reason and they are either here for a season to teach a valuable lesson in your life or they could be here for a lifetime. At the end of the day the choice is up to you where you want your future to lie. I had to learn the hard way and now my vision is more clear than it has ever been. I encourage everyone to complete college, follow your path that God has placed in your life, and leave the men alone; they will come in time. Don't fall in love too quickly and don't ever stop focusing on your dreams and goals. Become an aspiration to be an inspiration for others and spread that love. The world we live has changed over the years and we need to continue to keep our youth, as well as the next generation on that same path.

CHAPTER 10

What I Have Learned

Everyone makes their mistake and what matters most is we learn from them. I was supposed to go off to college to complete my degree, but as we all know life has obstacles and various challenges which led me to having little Christian, with no preparation for the future. I have no regrets because everything we go through is a lesson learned. The truth is while I was going through the issues with relationships and following my dreams, I would see a doctor about my illness, but not as often as I needed to. I stopped taking all medications because I felt there was no way it was progressing and no major differences in my joints. With a lot of research, I came to the conclusion that there were other ways to deal and cope with this illness. I started doing a lot more walking and various exercises to remain active and mobile. Eating healthier and being inspired to use the Nutri-bullet that contained fruits and vegetables that are filled with vitamins needed to control my inflammation. That's right! I started to self diagnose myself and knew what I had to do. Growing up, I have been through my ups and downs, but demand to continue to live a normal life regardless of my disability and other conditions. I never titled myself as being disabled, because I know there are other individuals who are far worse than I am and wish to have that typical lifestyle, but what a lot of individuals do not understand is that anything is possible; never give up. I am normal as the person reading this book. I carry the characteristics of being independent, and a strong-willed human being. I can do anything that other people can do and to many, even better. No one should feel put down because of the mistakes we make, but to just move forward and make the best of every situation. Do right by others and you will receive your reward along the way. Each day I prepare myself to fight arthritis and sometime arthritis may think it's won, but I battle it everyday. There are always going to be some good days and some days that are bad, but just don't give up or it will win. Keep pushing yourself and others to make the best of each situation. Thinking back on what my doctor told me and how it would be impossible for me to walk at the age of 15 and I would be in a wheelchair and to be standing here right now healthy and in charge of my own destiny, is a blessing! Life is a struggle, and we must prepare our mind and heart to fight arthritis or any other diseases that may be holding you back, but in reality it's all in the mind. Have you ever thought that the only thing holding you back is YOURSELF? I am determined to carry this to the finish line or I could just give up. We all know giving up is not an option for me and it shouldn't be for you. I choose to beat arthritis and not let it beat me; fight thru it and keep on going!

My weakness was allowing others to use me and abusing my intelligence and putting myself into deeper holes. My strengths have always been the dependency to strive towards my goals and dreaming of becoming the best of what I am and increasing those strengths 10 times more. I associate myself around great companions, who know a lot about my condition and who has seen my struggles being a single mother, and has continuously applaud me every step of the way, only because they have seen what I had to sacrifice to get this far. At the end of the day, I wouldn't trade any of this for the world, only because this was something I had to go through to get to where I am today. I only have one person to thank for this and that is the man above for showing me the way to my destiny. This is my introduction and my life as a child and learning what life decisions are all about as an adult. There are no shortcuts to be made, just focus on your biggest aspects and you will succeed. This is my story and there is still more to come and lessons that need to be learned, and with a simple push, there is no doubt that I won't get there, because *I know I can make it happen, Now it's your turn!*.

CHAPTER 11

(The Final Destination) My Career

I know where I have been and I definitely know where I am finally going. After the death of my cousin. It took awhile to get over that loss with the help of the speaker who helped me in getting through my pain and fear of moving forward. Around January 2015, I made a choice to further my career in event and wedding planning, but there was only one problem. I did not know where to start, so I spent more time doing research and trying to find out how to go about starting my own business and making it happen. This was my year and I finally felt that power surge running through me. My change is now and it was starting to happen: "Final Destination 2015."

My thought process started to change and everyone and everything that brought any negativity my way, I gained the courage to either ignore it or remove it out of my life. I needed help to start this business I wanted so badly to achieve. Everyday I was either thinking, researching, or dreaming about how I could make this business a reality. After a few months had rolled by, the business I so longed for continued to still stay stuck inside my head. I decided that I wanted to go to school to increase my knowledge and become a certified event and wedding planner. I researched a few event planning schools and there were some that were cheaper than others and much more affordable for my budget. I tried getting advice from others and some people had their own personal opinions, about which direction was the best step to take to starting my own business in events. I received opinions from family members who suggested that I should just work for an event planner instead of taking the courses in learning the right and productive way of knowing all about what being an event planner entails. Shortcuts don't work; I chose to learn the material so I could make the money I'm trying to make and develop the experience. It was a good idea, but it was not the greatest plan in my eyes. I did not want to take any shortcuts when it came to making the money I wanted to make to become successful. I know this was going to be a journey to get there and I was prepared for it. Shortcuts are also a way of taking the easy way out and one thing I have learned when starting your own business or attempting to, there are no such thing as shortcuts or quick money in that case. It takes hard work and dedication to get where you want to be; trust me, I never knew this until now.

There was an event planning school that was top notch, called QC School of Events and I was offered everything I needed to get my own business jumping very quickly. This is what I was looking for and it was $1500 to start the courses and well worth it. I asked some family members for the money to help pay for my online courses, but had no luck in getting help from anyone. I was not making enough to pay for the courses on my own, but I did have the option to pay in installments, which raised the full price of the courses to $1700. I did not feel like I had too much of a choice if I wanted to get ahead in my career. I had just turned 30 years old, April 20th and I had already felt as if I lost so much time and money over the years. I did not have much to pay for the courses at the time, but I chose to go for it with no regrets. Sometimes you have to just push yourself to do the positive, even if it is your last dollar. Talk about "determination."

I was excited, I finally did it! I received the email saying, "Welcome to QC School of Event and Wedding Planning." There was quite a few people who didn't believe I had what it took and had just given up on me. Some even thought that this was one of my dead end ideas and if there weren't thinking that; then, they just made me feel that way. The only one, who seen, and believed in me was my mother. My mother would show her support by helping me come up with these grand ideas on how far my business could go and where it could possibly expand to in the next 10 years or so. I had a vision and I seen what I needed to do and this was something I needed to invest in for myself. I made a commitment to not quit if things became too difficult to bare. This allowed me to stay motivated in going along with my plans. I learned if you have a dream that you know can make it; well, dream big and put it in gear no matter what the circumstances are.

I know I have made my mistakes, but I have always been goal driven. I just needed that voice in my head to finally embrace that transition. While I was taking these courses day by day and staying constantly on the computer and learning everything I needed to learn; A month later, I registered my own website: www.monaspartyplanning.net. I came up with the name Mona's Party Planning for my business, because that was my family name and it symbolized, the original Monalisa! I have dreams to take this business as far as the celebrity level and one day having my own brand, my own television show, as well as my own party supply stores in selected states. This is what God has been preparing me for and all the good that I have done for others was finally paying off. This was the beginning of where I needed to be in this point of my life and there was no stopping me. My mind is finally focused on my future, my son's future, and the future of my health and business. I am now a business woman; feels so good to have that type of mindset and finally ready to lift off.

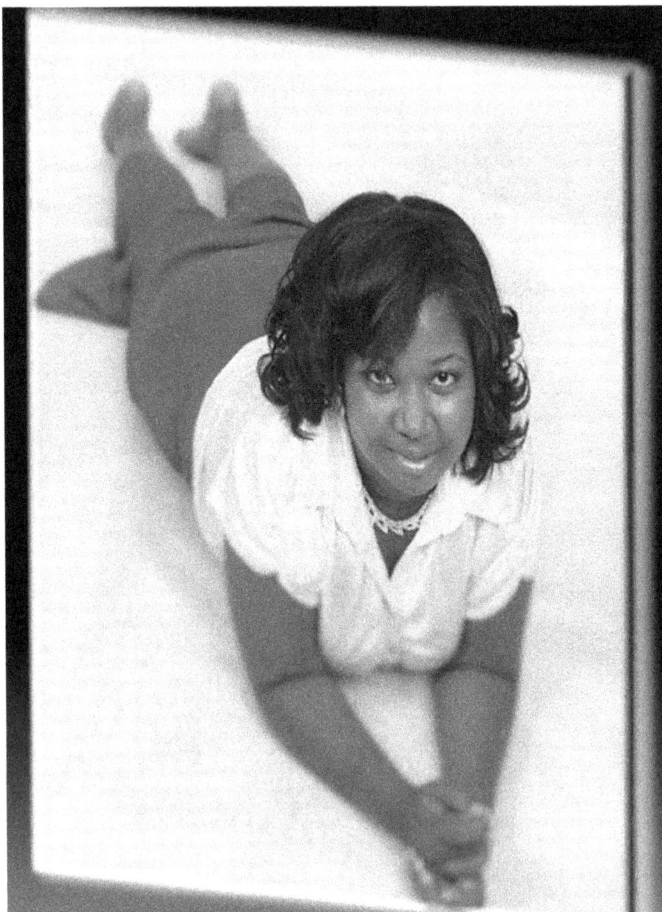

In life, we do a lot of *thinking* with no sense of urgency to back up what we so long for. As we continue to draw our thoughts to bring forth our mindsets; congrats! You have now begun to *dream*. It's now time to get a pen and paper to make your dream a *reality!* This is starting to make sense now, *Think.Dream.Reality.* Get it now? Or Are you still in the *dreaming* process? I know you're not in the *reality* stage because you continue to read as if you are curious to know more.

Coping with an illness that I allowed to take control of me as a child. At the time, I could not tell you what *"Think.Dream.Reality."* even meant, but to enjoy life; this was my motive at the age of six through college. While becoming a single mother, not knowing where my life was headed as I started contemplating if my life was over; falling into the worst situations and dead-end relationships. With the emotional hurt and pain, I begun to push forth my strengths and knock down my weaknesses. Only I could make a change. I woke up only to realize that I am stronger than I look and I can do anything that anyone else can do. *Believe* it and it can be done; now that's *Reality!*

—MONIQUE MCKENZIE—

Acknowledgements

I want to give thanks to the people who inspired me to be the woman I am today. First and foremost, I want to thank my mother, Maria Mckenzie for teaching me the aspects of life expectations and instilling the importance of education even when I was too stubborn to pay attention. Thank you mom for never giving up on me and being there to take great care of my illness to make sure I was able to live my life as normal as possible to the best of your ability. You deserve an honor award of being the best mom my sister, brother, and I, as well as other members in our family could ever have. You are the bridge that supports us and keep us from falling. Thank you for everything even if I never showed it. Me and you will always be and forever more!

Next, I want to give thanks to my aunt, Kimmy Alexandre. Although we butt heads often, my side you have never left. If I needed a place to stay you were there at my most desperate time, in addition to also showing tough love that empowered me to stand on my own two feet. It started since I was in high school and my mother moved away to New York. I went off to college and life started to happen and I got pregnant; you took me in every time, even with the mistakes that I had made of not completing my degree. I gave you the honor of naming my son, Jaden because of your support and care for us; not to mention you were there for the day of my delivery of my one and only son. I have always looked up to you, because you continued to go from career to career until you finally found your calling. I continually strive to do the same thing until now I have finally found what makes me happy all because of you. You are the one who made me stronger as a person and gave me the courage to keep going and never give up.

Shout out to my dear Godmother, Sherryl Soares, thank you for always being the rock for me and Jaden and being my second mother to make sure we were always taken care of and being there for us if we ever needed anything. I don't know where we would be right now if it wasn't for your love and moral support.

My church mom, Ms. Rebecca, thank you for always keeping me and my son in your prayers and making sure we continue to give praises to God for our blessings and our future blessings to come.

I want to give thanks to my friends and family who has seen my struggles as a single mother striving to provide the best support for my child's well being and for giving me the opportunity to become that inspirational icon, due to the fact of having the determination to succeed in everything I do.

I would also like to say thank you to my teachers, as well as, the clubs and organizations at Cinco Ranch High School, that I was involved in and for accepting me to find my individuality going through my most challenging times through school due to my illness.

Monique's Bonus Tips

Dealing with Stress

Stress can raise your blood pressure and can allow your joints to become inflamed

- Try and remain calm- I understand how difficult that can be depending on the situation
- X marks the spot- removing all negativity out of your life, including friends and family that may cause any drama
- Don't eat yourself away—please don't eat everything you see, it will blow you up without you even knowing
- Exercising keeps your stress level down—take a nice walk around your residence or at the track if you just want to get away.

Dealing with Depression

Depression and stress goes hand in hand.

- Feeling Sad- take a walk and enjoy the nice weather
- Talk to someone (family, friends, co-workers)
- Call the Suicide Hotline (1-800-273-8255)

- ❖ TEXT "GO" to 741-741 and a crisis counselor will answer all questions
- ❖ Stay calm-have faith-keep pushing forth and just know that overtime it will go away

Dealing with Fatigue

Do not overwork your body- it can cause stiffness in joints

- ❖ Get plenty of rest- just like our body needs food for energy, the same with REST
- ❖ Make a fruit and vegetable smoothie (ex:nutri-bullet)
- ❖ Take your vitamins regularly
- ❖ Do not eat excessively

Signs to know that a Flare is on its way

- ❖ Stiffness in joints
- ❖ Pain in joints
- ❖ Limited flexibility
- ❖ Night Sweats
- ❖ Joints feel warm (inflamed)
- ❖ Swelling of joints

Tips on Healthy Joints
- ❖ All of the Above

Please note: This is only based on the author's experience